roasted

everyone's favourite meal

Women's Weekly
THE AUSTRALIAN

contents

AUSTRALIAN CUP AND
SPOON MEASUREMENTS
ARE METRIC.
A CONVERSION CHART
APPEARS ON PAGE 77.

Roasts are easy to prepare, nutritious, and
great for feeding large numbers (or creating
leftovers for school lunches). Remember to
allow time for your roast to rest before serving.
A resting time of 10-20 minutes is crucial as
it allows the meat juices to settle - resulting in
more tender, delicious meat.

Pamela Clark

Food Director

beef & veal

ROASTED BEEF FILLET WITH HORSERADISH MAYONNAISE

prep + cook time 1 hour (+ standing) **serves** 6
nutritional count per serving 45.8g total fat (9.7g saturated fat); 2792kJ (668 cal);
22.6g carbohydrate; 40.4g protein; 3.5g fibre

2 bunches fresh thyme
1kg (2-pound) piece beef eye fillet
2 tablespoons olive oil
1 teaspoon coarsely ground black pepper
horseradish mayonnaise
2 egg yolks
2 tablespoons lemon juice
¾ cup (180ml) olive oil
1 tablespoon prepared horseradish
2 tablespoons finely chopped fresh chives

1 Preheat oven to 220°C/425°F. Cover base of large shallow baking dish with thyme.
2 Trim excess fat from beef; tie with kitchen string at 2.5cm (1-inch) intervals. Brush beef all over with a little of the oil, sprinkle with pepper.
3 Cook beef in heated large frying pan until browned all over; place on thyme in baking dish. Roast, uncovered, 30 minutes or until beef is cooked as desired.
4 Meanwhile, make horseradish mayonnaise.

5 Remove beef from dish; discard thyme. Cover; stand 10 minutes before carving.
6 Serve beef with horseradish mayonnaise.
horseradish mayonnaise Blend egg yolks and juice until smooth. With motor operating, add oil in a thin, steady stream until mayonnaise thickens. Add horseradish; blend until combined. Transfer to medium bowl; stir in chives. Adjust consistency by stirring in a little hot water. Cover; refrigerate until required.
tip Homemade mayonnaise is not hard to make, and it's well worth the effort. If time is short, buy a good-quality whole-egg mayonnaise and flavour it to your taste with some lemon juice, prepared horseradish and finely chopped chives.
serving suggestion Serve with roasted potatoes and steamed peas.

VEAL SHANKS WITH HONEY AND LEMON

prep + cook time 4 hours 35 minutes **serves** 4
nutritional count per serving 11.3g total fat (4.1g saturated fat); 1562kJ (467 cal);
24.9g carbohydrate; 61.7g protein; 1.4g fibre

30g (1 ounce) butter, softened
4 french-trimmed veal shanks (2kg)
1 medium lemon (140g), quartered
⅓ cup (115g) honey
4 cloves garlic
⅓ cup (80ml) dry white wine
⅓ cup (80ml) veal or beef stock

1 Preheat oven to 160°C/325°F.
2 Grease four 30cm x 40cm (12-inch x 16-inch) pieces of baking paper with butter; place one shank on each piece of paper. Top each shank with a lemon quarter, 1 tablespoon of the honey and one crushed garlic clove. Stand shanks upright, enclose with paper; tie loosely with kitchen string. Carefully pour a little of the combined wine and stock into each package; tighten string to secure firmly.
3 Stand packages in small deep casserole dish, so they fit snugly. Cover; roast 4 hours.
4 Serve shanks in their packages, to be opened at the table.
serving suggestion Serve with mashed potato and steamed green vegetables.

VITELLO TONNATO

prep + cook time 1 hour 20 minutes serves 4
nutritional count per serving 55.4g total fat (13g saturated fat); 3219kJ (770 cal);
23.5g carbohydrate; 44.2g protein; 1.6g fibre

10g (½ ounce) butter, softened
600g (1¼-pound) veal rump
40g (1½ ounces) butter, melted
1 tablespoon finely chopped fresh sage
185g (6 ounces) canned tuna in olive oil,
    drained, flaked
1 tablespoon drained capers, rinsed
4 drained anchovy fillets
1½ cups (450g) whole-egg mayonnaise
2 teaspoons lemon juice
80g (2½ ounces) baby rocket (arugula) leaves
6 cherry truss tomatoes (120g), halved
1 medium lemon (140g), cut into wedges

1 Preheat oven to 200°C/400°F.
2 Grease 25cm x 30cm (10-inch x 12-inch)
piece of foil with softened butter. Season
veal; wrap in foil. Place veal on wire rack in
large baking dish; roast about 1 hour or until
cooked as desired, basting every 20 minutes
with combined melted butter and sage.
Remove veal from oven; stand 10 minutes.
3 Meanwhile, blend or process tuna,
capers, anchovies, mayonnaise and juice
until smooth.
4 Slice veal thinly. Arrange veal on platter with
rocket, tomato, and lemon; drizzle with ¾ cup
tuna dressing. Serve with remaining dressing;
sprinkle with extra capers, if you like.
tip Vitello tonnato, veal with tuna sauce, is
a classic Italian antipasto dish, usually
served cold. It's also commonly served in
summer as a light meal.

SIRLOIN ROAST WITH HERB STUFFING

prep + cook time 1 hour 50 minutes **serves** 8
nutritional count per serving 32.9g total fat (14g saturated fat); 2700kJ (646 cal);
12.6g carbohydrate; 73g protein; 1.1g fibre

2.5kg (5-pound) boneless beef sirloin roast
2 tablespoons olive oil
2 tablespoons plain (all-purpose) flour
⅓ cup (80ml) dry red wine
1½ cups (375ml) beef stock
herb stuffing
45g (1½ ounces) butter
2 rindless bacon slices (130g),
    chopped finely
1 medium brown onion (150g),
    chopped finely
1 clove garlic, crushed
1½ cups (105g) stale breadcrumbs
½ cup (40g) coarsely grated
    parmesan cheese
1 egg
1 tablespoon wholegrain mustard
2 tablespoons each finely chopped fresh
    oregano and flat-leaf parsley
2 teaspoons finely grated lemon rind

1 Make herb stuffing.
2 Preheat oven to 220°C/425°F.
3 Cut between fat and meat of beef, making a pocket for stuffing; trim and discard a little of the fat. Spoon stuffing into pocket; lay fat over stuffing to enclose. Tie beef with kitchen string at 2cm (¾-inch) intervals; place beef on wire rack over shallow large baking dish. Drizzle with oil.
4 Roast beef, uncovered, about 1½ hours. Remove beef from dish; cover with foil, stand 10 minutes.
5 Reserve 2 tablespoons of beef juices in baking dish; place over heat. Add flour; cook, stirring, until mixture thickens and bubbles. Gradually add wine and stock, stirring, until gravy boils and thickens slightly.
6 Slice beef thinly. Serve with gravy.
herb stuffing Melt butter in medium frying pan; cook bacon, onion and garlic, stirring, until onion softens. Cool. Combine bacon mixture with remaining ingredients in bowl.
serving suggestion Serve with your choice of roasted vegetables.

ROAST BEEF WITH YORKSHIRE PUDDINGS

prep + cook time 2 hours 35 minutes (+ refrigeration & standing) **serves** 8
nutritional count per serving 15.4g total fat (4.8g saturated fat); 2169kJ (519 cal);
21.1g carbohydrate; 61.2g protein; 4g fibre

2kg (4-pound) corner piece
   beef topside roast
2 cups (500ml) dry red wine
¼ cup (70g) wholegrain mustard
4 cloves garlic, sliced
2 bay leaves
6 black peppercorns
4 sprigs fresh thyme
1 medium brown onion (150g),
   chopped coarsely
2 medium carrots (240g), chopped coarsely
1 large leek (500g), chopped coarsely
2 stalks celery (300g), trimmed,
   chopped coarsely
2 tablespoons olive oil
yorkshire pudding batter
1 cup (150g) plain (all-purpose) flour
2 eggs
½ cup (125ml) milk
½ cup (125ml) water
gravy
2 tablespoons plain (all-purpose) flour
1½ cups (375ml) beef stock

1 Combine beef, wine, mustard, garlic, bay leaves, peppercorns, thyme and onion in large shallow dish. Cover; refrigerate 3 hours or overnight.
2 Preheat oven to 180°C/350°F.
3 Drain beef over medium bowl; reserve 1 cup of marinade. Combine carrot, leek and celery in large baking dish, top with beef; brush beef with oil. Roast beef, uncovered, about 1½ hours.

4 Meanwhile, make yorkshire pudding batter.
5 Remove dish from oven. Increase oven to 220°C/425°F. Wrap beef in foil; stand 30 minutes or until ready to serve.
6 Remove vegetables from dish with slotted spoon; discard vegetables. Pour pan juices into jug; stand 2 minutes. Reserve 1½ tablespoons oil from the surface for yorkshire puddings, discard remaining surface oil; reserve 2 tablespoons of the pan juices for gravy.
7 Spoon reserved oil into eight holes of 12-hole (⅓-cup/80ml) muffin pan; heat in oven 2 minutes. Spoon yorkshire pudding batter into pan holes. Bake about 20 minutes or until puffed and golden.
8 Meanwhile, make gravy.
9 Serve beef with yorkshire puddings and gravy.
yorkshire pudding batter Sift flour into medium bowl; whisk in combined eggs, milk and the water all at once until smooth. Stand batter 30 minutes.
gravy Heat reserved pan juices in same baking dish, add flour; cook, stirring, until browned. Gradually add stock and reserved marinade; cook, stirring, until mixture boils and thickens. Strain gravy into heatproof jug.
serving suggestion Serve the beef and yorkshire puddings with your choice of vegetables.

BEEF RIB ROAST WITH SPICED SALT

prep + cook time 1 hour 50 minutes (+ standing) **serves** 4
nutritional count per serving 62.6g total fat (18.3g saturated fat); 4468kJ (1069 cal);
14.5g carbohydrate; 112.4g protein; 0.7g fibre

1 tablespoon each coriander seeds and
    cumin seeds
½ cup (60g) sea salt flakes
¼ teaspoon mixed spice
1 teaspoon freshly ground pepper
3kg (6-pound) beef standing rib roast
1 tablespoon olive oil
garlic mayonnaise
1 cup (300g) whole-egg mayonnaise
1 tablespoon water
2 teaspoons lemon juice
2 cloves garlic, crushed
1 teaspoon dijon mustard

1 Preheat oven to 200°C/400°F.
2 Using a mortar and pestle, grind the
seeds together until coarsely crushed.
Add salt, mixed spice and pepper; mix well.
Remove a third of the spice mixture and
reserve. Brush beef with oil, rub remaining
spice mixture all over beef.
3 Roast beef, uncovered, about 1½ hours
(for rare), or until cooked as desired. Cover;
stand 15 minutes before carving.
4 Meanwhile, dry-fry reserved spice mix in
small frying pan, stirring over low heat about
1 minute or until fragrant. Cool.
5 Make garlic mayonnaise.
6 Serve beef with mayonnaise and toasted
spice mix.
garlic mayonnaise Combine ingredients in
a small bowl.

SLOW-COOKED BEEF POT ROAST

prep + cook time 8 hours 30 minutes **serves** 4
nutritional count per serving 26.8g total fat (7.5g saturated fat); 2353kJ (563 cal);
25g carbohydrate; 46.8g protein; 7.1g fibre

¼ cup (60ml) olive oil
4 small potatoes (180g), unpeeled, halved
375g (12-ounce) piece unpeeled pumpkin,
    cut into four wedges
8 baby onions (200g), halved
375g (12 ounces) baby carrots, trimmed
250g (8 ounces) jerusalem
    artichokes (sunchokes)
750g (1½-pound) piece beef blade steak
1 tablespoon wholegrain mustard
2 teaspoons smoked paprika
2 teaspoons finely chopped fresh rosemary
1 clove garlic, crushed
1½ cups (375ml) beef stock
½ cup (125ml) dry red wine
2 tablespoons balsamic vinegar
¼ cup (35g) gravy powder
2 tablespoons water

1 Heat 2 tablespoons of the oil in large frying pan; cook potato, pumpkin and onion, in batches, until browned all over. Place vegetables in 4.5-litre (18-cup) slow cooker with carrots and artichokes.
2 Heat 2 teaspoons of the remaining oil in same pan; cook beef until browned all over. Remove beef from pan; spread with combined mustard, paprika, rosemary, garlic and remaining oil.
3 Place beef on vegetables in slow cooker; pour over combined stock, wine and vinegar. Cook, covered, on low, 8 hours.
4 Remove beef and vegetables from cooker; cover beef, stand 10 minutes before slicing thinly. Cover vegetables to keep warm.
5 Meanwhile, combine gravy powder with the water in small bowl until smooth. Stir gravy mixture into liquid in slow cooker; cook, covered, on high, about 10 minutes or until gravy has thickened slightly. Season to taste. Strain gravy.
6 Serve beef with vegetables and gravy.
tips We used nicola potatoes and jap pumpkin in this recipe. Jerusalem artichokes can be hard to find – you can leave them out and add swede, parsnip or turnip to the pot roast instead. Gravy powder is an instant gravy mix made with browned flour. Plain (all-purpose) flour can be used for thickening instead.
serving suggestion Serve with steamed green beans or broccoli.

BEEF WELLINGTON WITH CAULIFLOWER PUREE

prep + cook time 1 hour 45 minutes (+ standing) **serves** 4
nutritional count per serving 58.2g total fat (18.3g saturated fat); 3586kJ (858 cal);
35.8g carbohydrate; 45.8g protein; 6.1g fibre

500g (1-pound) piece beef eye fillet
2 tablespoons olive oil
1 tablespoon cumin seeds
10g (½ ounce) dried porcini mushrooms
1 cup (250ml) boiling water
20g (¾ ounce) butter
1 shallot (25g), chopped finely
200g (6½ ounces) button mushrooms,
    chopped coarsely
2 tablespoons (40g) duck liver pâté
1 tablespoon each finely chopped fresh
    flat-leaf parsley and fresh chervil
6 silver beet (swiss chard) leaves (390g),
    trimmed
6 slices prosciutto (90g)
2 sheets puff pastry
1 egg, beaten lightly
1 teaspoon cumin seeds, extra
40g (1½ ounces) butter, extra
¼ cup (60ml) water
1 small brown onion (80g), sliced thinly
½ cauliflower (500g), chopped coarsely
2 tablespoons pouring cream

1 Rub beef with oil, sprinkle with cumin;
season. Cook beef in heated large frying
pan, turning, until browned all over. Remove
from heat; place on wire rack over tray.
Cover; refrigerate until cool.
2 Meanwhile, combine porcini mushrooms
and the boiling water in small heatproof
bowl. Cover; stand 10 minutes, drain.
3 Heat butter in large frying pan; cook
shallot, stirring, until softened. Add button
mushrooms; cook, stirring, about 5 minutes

or until softened. Process porcini mushrooms,
button mushroom mixture and pâté, pulsing,
until finely chopped. Stir in herbs; cool.
4 Cook silver beet in medium saucepan of
boiling water about 30 seconds or until
pliable; drain well on absorbent paper.
5 Place a large oven tray in the oven.
Preheat oven to 210°C/410°F.
6 Lay silver beet, overlapping slightly, on
board to make 25cm x 35cm (10-inch x
14-inch) rectangle. Top with prosciutto,
overlapping slightly; spread evenly with
mushroom mixture. Place beef along one
long side; roll silver beet to enclose beef.
7 Cut 10cm x 15cm (4-inch x 6-inch)
rectangle from one sheet of pastry; lay on
top of beef. Place beef in centre of remaining
pastry sheet. Cut four corners out of the
pastry, in line with the beef. Lift up sides of
pastry around beef, pressing to seal.
8 Place beef, seam-side down, on heated
oven tray. Cut 1cm (½-inch) round from top
of pastry. Brush pastry with egg; sprinkle
with extra cumin seeds. Bake, uncovered,
about 35 minutes. Cover; stand 15 minutes
before slicing.
9 Meanwhile, heat extra butter and the
water in medium saucepan, add onion and
cauliflower; cook, covered, over low heat,
stirring occasionally, about 30 minutes or
until very soft. Cool 10 minutes. Blend or
process cauliflower mixture with cream until
smooth; season to taste.
10 Serve beef wellington with warmed
cauliflower puree.

lamb

LAMB BRETONNE

prep + cook time 2 hours 30 minutes **serves** 4
nutritional count per serving 19.9g total fat (9.5g saturated fat); 2324kJ (556 cal);
20.2g carbohydrate; 69.8g protein; 7.7g fibre

1.5kg (3-pound) leg of lamb
1 clove garlic, sliced thinly
2 sprigs fresh rosemary
1 teaspoon sea salt flakes
½ teaspoon freshly cracked black pepper
20g (¾ ounce) butter
2 medium brown onions (300g), sliced thinly
3 cloves garlic, crushed
410g (13 ounces) canned crushed tomatoes
410g (13 ounces) canned tomato puree
2 cups (500ml) beef stock
410g (13 ounces) canned white beans,
    drained, rinsed

1 Preheat oven to 180°C/350°F.
2 Trim excess fat from lamb. Pierce lamb in several places with sharp knife; press sliced garlic and a little of the rosemary firmly into cuts. Rub salt and pepper over lamb.
3 Heat butter in large flameproof baking dish; cook onion and crushed garlic, stirring, until onion browns slightly. Stir in undrained tomatoes, puree, stock, beans and remaining rosemary; bring to the boil, then remove from heat.
4 Place lamb, pierced-side down, on bean mixture, cover; transfer to oven. Cook 1 hour. Turn lamb carefully; cook, uncovered, brushing occasionally with tomato mixture, about 1 hour or until lamb is cooked to your liking.

ROLLED LAMB LOIN WITH TOMATO CONCASSE

prep + cook time 2 hours **serves** 4
nutritional count per serving 22.8g total fat (6.6g saturated fat); 1894kJ (453 cal);
5g carbohydrate; 54.9g protein; 3.2g fibre

1 medium red capsicum (bell pepper) (200g)
750g (1½-pound) boned loin of lamb
2 cloves garlic, crushed
20g (¾ ounce) baby spinach leaves
⅓ cup loosely packed fresh basil leaves
1 tablespoon olive oil
tomato concasse
1 tablespoon olive oil
3 shallots (75g), chopped finely
4 cloves garlic, crushed
1.2kg (2½ pounds) large egg (plum)
    tomatoes, peeled, seeded, chopped finely
2 tablespoons red wine vinegar

1 Preheat oven to 240°C/475°F.
2 Make tomato concasse.
3 Meanwhile, quarter capsicum; discard seeds and membranes. Roast, skin-side up, in oven until skin blisters and blackens. Cover capsicum in plastic wrap 5 minutes; peel away skin, then slice capsicum thinly.
4 Reduce oven to 180°C/350°F. Place lamb, cut-side up, on board; rub garlic into lamb. Place capsicum, spinach and basil down centre of lamb; roll tightly, securing at 2cm (¾-inch) intervals with kitchen string. Rub oil over lamb roll.
5 Place lamb on oiled wire rack over large shallow baking dish; roast, uncovered, about 1 hour or until lamb is browned and cooked as desired. Cover lamb; stand 10 minutes before slicing.
6 Serve thick slices of lamb with warm tomato concasse.
tomato concasse Heat oil in medium saucepan; cook shallot and garlic, stirring, until shallot softens. Add tomato and vinegar; cook, covered, over low heat, 15 minutes. Uncover; simmer, stirring occasionally, about 30 minutes or until mixture thickens slightly.
serving suggestion Serve with peas.

MEXICAN SLOW-ROASTED LAMB SHANKS

prep + cook time 8 hours 30 minutes **serves** 4
nutritional count per serving 14.1g total fat (3.5g saturated fat); 1659kJ (397 cal);
4.2g carbohydrate; 61.9g protein; 2g fibre

2 medium tomatoes (300g),
   chopped coarsely
1 medium red capsicum (bell pepper) (200g),
   chopped coarsely
1 medium yellow capsicum (bell pepper)
   (200g), chopped coarsely
2 tablespoons olive oil
2 teaspoons sweet paprika
2 teaspoons ground cumin
1 teaspoon ground coriander
2 cloves garlic, crushed
1 fresh long red chilli, chopped finely
2 tablespoons finely chopped fresh oregano
8 french-trimmed lamb shanks (2kg)

1 Combine tomato and capsicum in 4.5-litre (18-cup) slow cooker.
2 Combine oil, spices, garlic, chilli and oregano in large bowl; add lamb, turn to coat in marinade. Cook lamb in heated large frying pan, in batches, until browned. Transfer to cooker. Cook, covered, on low, 8 hours.
3 Serve lamb shanks drizzled with sauce; sprinkle with extra oregano leaves.
tip Lamb can be marinated in the spice mixture overnight, if you like.
serving suggestion Serve with flour tortillas, lime wedges and a mixed green salad.

SPICED LAMB ROAST WITH FIGS AND HONEY

prep + cook time 1 hour 50 minutes **serves** 6
nutritional count per serving 24.3g total fat (8.4g saturated fat); 2115kJ (506 cal);
15.6g carbohydrate; 55.6g protein; 2.9g fibre

3 cloves garlic, chopped finely
4cm (1½-inch) piece fresh ginger (20g), grated
2 fresh long red chillies, chopped finely
⅓ cup each finely chopped fresh flat-leaf
    parsley and fresh coriander (cilantro)
2 teaspoons each ground coriander
    and ground cumin
¼ cup (60ml) olive oil
2kg (4-pound) leg of lamb
9 medium fresh figs (540g), halved
2 tablespoons honey

1 Preheat oven to 180°C/350°F.
2 Combine garlic, ginger, chilli, herbs, spices and oil in small bowl.
3 Rub herb mixture all over lamb. Place lamb in oiled large baking dish; roast, uncovered, 1¼ hours.
4 Add figs to dish; drizzle honey over figs and lamb. Roast about 15 minutes or until lamb is cooked as desired. Cover lamb; stand 10 minutes before slicing.
5 Serve lamb with figs.
serving suggestion Serve with couscous.

SALT-BAKED LAMB
WITH LEMON AND ARTICHOKE SAUCE

prep + cook time 1 hour 25 minutes (+ refrigeration) **serves** 4
nutritional count per serving 39g total fat (20.7g saturated fat); 2550kJ (610 cal);
7.2g carbohydrate; 54.7g protein; 1.1g fibre

1 teaspoon fennel seeds
1 clove garlic, crushed
1.3kg (2¾-pound) easy carve leg of lamb
1 tablespoon olive oil
2 cups (500g) coarse cooking salt
   (kosher salt)
1½ cups (375ml) water
3⅓ cups (500g) plain (all-purpose) flour
1 sprig fresh rosemary
3 thin slices lemon
1 tablespoon fresh rosemary leaves
lemon and artichoke sauce
30g (1 ounce) butter
2 tablespoons plain (all-purpose) flour
1 cup (250ml) vegetable stock
¼ cup (60ml) dry white wine
2 teaspoons finely grated lemon rind
¼ cup (60ml) lemon juice
8 drained marinated artichoke hearts (100g),
   chopped coarsely
½ cup (125ml) pouring cream

1 Combine fennel seeds and garlic in small bowl. Press mixture all over lamb. Heat oil in large frying pan; cook lamb, turning, until browned all over. Transfer lamb to wire rack over tray. Cover; refrigerate until cool.
2 Meanwhile, combine salt and water in large bowl; stir in flour until combined and becomes a soft, smooth dough. Wrap in plastic; refrigerate 30 minutes.
3 Preheat oven to 250°C/480°F.
4 Roll dough on floured surface until 5mm (¼ inch) thick. Place rosemary sprig, then lemon slices along centre of dough; top with lamb. Fold dough over lamb to enclose; place seam-side down on baking paper lined oven tray. Roast, uncovered, 45 minutes. Remove from oven; stand lamb, in crust, 15 minutes, then break crust open and remove lamb.
5 Meanwhile, make lemon and artichoke sauce.
6 Serve sliced lamb with rosemary and sauce.

lemon and artichoke sauce Melt butter in medium saucepan, add flour; cook, stirring, until mixture thickens and bubbles. Gradually add stock and wine; cook, stirring, about 10 minutes or until sauce boils and thickens. Stir in rind, juice, artichoke and cream; cook, stirring until hot.

PISTACHIO AND OLIVE STUFFED LAMB FOREQUARTER WITH BEETROOT SALAD

prep + cook time 2 hours (+ standing) **serves** 4
nutritional count per serving 38.9g total fat (17g saturated fat); 3892kJ (931 cal);
67.5g carbohydrate; 72.5g protein; 11.3g fibre

1 cup (200g) couscous
1¼ cups (310ml) boiling water
10g (½ ounce) butter
1½ tablespoons unsalted, roasted, shelled
  pistachios, chopped finely
20g (¾ ounce) haloumi cheese,
  chopped finely
1 teaspoon finely grated lemon rind
1 tablespoon finely chopped seeded
  green olives
1 fresh small green chilli, chopped finely
2 teaspoons finely chopped fresh
  flat-leaf parsley
1kg (2-pound) boneless lamb forequarter
2 tablespoons olive oil
¼ cup loosely packed fresh flat-leaf
  parsley leaves
3 medium beetroot (beets) (1.5kg),
  peeled, chopped coarsely
180g (5½ ounces) persian fetta cheese,
  drained
1 medium lemon (140g), cut into wedges

1 Combine couscous and the boiling water in medium heatproof bowl, cover; stand 5 minutes or until water is absorbed, fluffing with fork occasionally. Stir in butter.
2 Preheat oven to 210°C/410°F.
3 Combine ¼ cup couscous mixture, nuts, haloumi, rind, olives, chilli, and chopped parsley in small bowl. Open lamb out flat. Press couscous mixture along one long side of lamb; roll lamb to enclose filling. Tie roll with kitchen string, at 2cm (¾-inch) intervals, to secure. Rub lamb with half the oil.
4 Place lamb on oiled wire rack in large shallow baking dish; roast 30 minutes.
5 Meanwhile, combine beetroot with remaining oil in medium bowl. Place in small shallow baking dish. Reduce oven to 180°C/350°F; roast beetroot alongside lamb about 45 minutes or until beetroot is tender and lamb is cooked as desired.
6 Remove lamb from oven, cover; stand 15 minutes before slicing.
7 Meanwhile, combine remaining couscous and parsley leaves in medium bowl. Combine beetroot and fetta in another medium bowl.
8 Serve sliced lamb with couscous and beetroot salad.

poultry

ROASTED HARISSA CHICKEN

prep + cook time 1 hour 35 minutes (+ refrigeration) **serves** 4
nutritional count per serving 47.4g total fat (13g saturated fat); 2968kJ (710 cal); 19.6g carbohydrate; 48.1g protein; 8.4g fibre

1.8kg (3¾-pound) whole chicken
¾ cup (225g) harissa
1 large carrot (180g), halved lengthways
1 large red onion (300g), quartered
2 stalks celery (300g), trimmed
10 sprigs (20g) fresh lemon thyme
1 medium garlic bulb (70g),
    halved crossways
2 tablespoons olive oil

1 Rinse chicken under cold water; pat dry inside and out with absorbent paper. Tuck wing tips under chicken. Brush harissa all over chicken; tie legs together with kitchen string. Cover; refrigerate 3 hours or overnight.
2 Preheat oven to 200°C/400°F.
3 Combine remaining ingredients in large shallow baking dish; top with chicken, season.
4 Roast chicken and vegetables about 1¼ hours or until chicken is cooked through. Cover; stand 10 minutes before serving.

CHICKEN POT ROAST
WITH MUSTARD CREAM SAUCE

prep + cook time 2 hours 15 minutes **serves** 4
nutritional count per serving 42.2g total fat (13.8g saturated fat); 2859kJ (684 cal);
16.9g carbohydrate; 46.7g protein; 6.6g fibre

1.6kg (3¼-pound) whole chicken
1 tablespoon olive oil
12 shallots (300g), halved
20 baby carrots (400g), trimmed
3 small parsnips (360g), chopped coarsely
1 cup (250ml) dry white wine
2 cups (500ml) chicken stock
2 dried bay leaves
200g (6½ ounces) swiss brown mushrooms
2 tablespoons pouring cream
2 tablespoons wholegrain mustard

1 Preheat oven to 200°C/400°F.
2 Wash chicken under cold water; pat dry inside and out with absorbent paper.
3 Heat oil in large flameproof casserole dish; cook chicken until browned all over. Remove chicken.
4 Cook shallot, carrots and parsnip in same dish over heat, stirring, about 5 minutes or until vegetables are browned lightly.
5 Return chicken to dish with wine, stock and bay leaves; bring to the boil. Cook, covered, in oven 30 minutes. Uncover; cook about 30 minutes or until chicken is cooked through. Add mushrooms; cook, uncovered, about 10 minutes or until mushrooms are tender. Remove chicken and vegetables from dish; cover to keep warm.
6 Add cream and mustard to dish; bring to the boil. Boil, uncovered, about 5 minutes or until sauce thickens slightly.
7 Serve chicken, cut into pieces, with vegetables and mustard cream sauce.
tip Swiss brown mushrooms (also called roman or cremini) are light-to-dark brown in colour with a full-bodied flavour. Store on a tray in a single layer, covered with damp absorbent paper, and keep where cool air can circulate around them.

ROASTED TURKEY
WITH FORCEMEAT STUFFING

prep + cook time 3 hours 45 minutes (+ cooling & standing) **serves** 8
nutritional count per serving 54.7g total fat (21g saturated fat); 3641kJ (871 cal);
12.8g carbohydrate; 79.6g protein; 1.4g fibre

4.5kg (9-pound) whole turkey
1 cup (250ml) water
80g (2½ ounces) butter, melted
¼ cup (35g) plain (all-purpose) flour
3 cups (750ml) chicken stock
½ cup (125ml) dry white wine
forcemeat stuffing
40g (1½ ounces) butter
3 medium brown onions (450g),
    chopped finely
2 rindless bacon slices (130g),
    chopped coarsely
1 cup (70g) fresh breadcrumbs
½ cup coarsely chopped fresh
    flat-leaf parsley
250g (8 ounces) minced (ground) pork
250g (8 ounces) minced (ground) chicken

1 Preheat oven to 180°C/350°F.
2 Make forcemeat stuffing.
3 Discard neck from turkey. Rinse turkey under cold water; pat dry inside and out with absorbent paper. Fill neck cavity loosely with stuffing; secure skin over opening with small skewers. Fill large cavity loosely with remaining stuffing; tie legs together with kitchen string.
4 Place turkey on oiled wire rack in large shallow baking dish; pour the water into dish. Brush turkey all over with half the butter; cover turkey tightly with two layers of greased foil. Roast 2 hours. Uncover turkey; brush with remaining butter. Roast, uncovered, about 1 hour or until cooked through. Remove turkey from dish, cover loosely with foil; stand 20 minutes.
5 Pour juice from dish into large jug; skim 1 tablespoon of fat from juice, return fat to same dish. Skim and discard fat from remaining juice; reserve juice. Add flour to dish; cook, stirring, until mixture bubbles and is well-browned. Gradually stir in stock, wine and reserved juice; cook, stirring, until gravy boils and thickens. Strain gravy into jug.
6 Serve turkey with gravy.

forcemeat stuffing Melt butter in medium frying pan; cook onion and bacon, stirring, over low heat until onion is soft. Cool. Combine onion mixture and remaining ingredients in large bowl.

tip To test if the turkey is cooked, insert a skewer sideways into the thickest part of the thigh, then remove and press flesh to release the juices. If the juice runs clear, the turkey is cooked. Alternatively, insert a meat thermometer into the thickest part of the thigh, without touching the bone; the turkey is cooked when the thermometer reaches 90°C/195°F.

ORANGE AND FIVE-SPICE CRISPY SKIN DUCK

prep + cook time 2 hours (+ refrigeration) **serves** 4
nutritional count per serving 99.4g total fat (29.6g saturated fat); 4510kJ (1079 cal);
21.9g carbohydrate; 35.1g protein; 3.2g fibre

1.8kg (3½-pound) whole duck
3 large oranges (900g), halved
2 fresh bay leaves
4 cinnamon sticks
1½ tablespoons salt
3 teaspoons five-spice powder
1 tablespoon olive oil

1 Rinse duck under cold water; pat dry inside and out with absorbent paper. Place duck in shallow dish. Cut one orange half into quarters; push orange quarters, one bay leaf and one cinnamon stick into duck cavity. Tie legs together with kitchen string; tuck wing tips under duck.
2 Combine salt and five-spice in small bowl. Rub duck with oil, then half the salt mixture. Cover; refrigerate 3 hours.
3 Preheat oven to 200°C/400°F.
4 Place remaining bay leaf, cinnamon and orange halves cut-side down, on rack in large shallow baking dish; place duck, breast-side down, on top. Roast, uncovered, 1¾ hours, turning duck and oranges every 30 minutes. Serve duck with reserved salt mixture.
serving suggestion Serve with steamed asian greens.

SPICED ROASTED CHICKENS WITH CORIANDER

prep + cook time 50 minutes (+ refrigeration) serves 4
nutritional count per serving 52.6g total fat (17.6g saturated fat); 2859kJ (684 cal);
1.5g carbohydrate; 51.5g protein; 1.7g fibre

4 small chickens (poussin) (2kg)
4 cloves garlic, peeled
4cm (1½-inch) piece fresh ginger (20g), grated
⅓ cup (40g) ground almonds
¼ cup (60ml) lemon juice
3 fresh coriander (cilantro) roots
½ teaspoon ground turmeric
3 teaspoons garam masala
3 fresh large green chillies, chopped coarsely
2 teaspoons salt
30g (1 ounce) ghee (clarified butter), melted
¼ cup firmly packed fresh coriander
   (cilantro) leaves

1 Place chickens on cutting board, cut down both sides of the backbones with poultry shears or sharp knife; remove and discard the backbones. Rinse cavity of each chicken and pat dry with absorbent paper. Place each chicken, breast-side up, on board; press the breastbone firmly with the heel of hand to flatten.

2 Blend or process garlic, ginger, ground almonds, juice, coriander roots, turmeric, garam masala, chilli and salt until combined. Rub spice mixture over chickens. Cover; refrigerate 3 hours or overnight.

3 Preheat oven to 240°C/475°F.

4 Place chickens on an oiled wire rack over large, shallow flameproof baking dish; brush with ghee. Roast, uncovered, about 30 minutes or until browned all over and cooked through.

5 Serve chickens with coriander leaves and lemon wedges, if you like.

tip In Australia, young, small chickens, weighing between 300g (9½ ounces) and 600g (1¼ pounds), are called spatchcocks. In other countries, they're called poussins, rock cornish hens or simply baby chickens.

ROASTED CHICKEN
WITH 40 CLOVES OF GARLIC

prep + cook time 1 hour 40 minutes (+ standing) **serves** 4
nutritional count per serving 45g total fat (17.9g saturated fat); 3219kJ (770 cal);
38.4g carbohydrate; 46.8g protein; 14.1g fibre

3 bulbs garlic
60g (2 ounces) butter, softened
1.5kg (3-pound) whole chicken
2 teaspoons salt
2 teaspoons cracked black pepper
1 cup (250ml) water

1 Preheat oven to 200°C/400°F.

2 Separate cloves from garlic bulbs, leaving peel intact. Rub butter over outside of chicken and inside cavity; press combined salt and pepper onto skin and inside cavity. Place half the garlic inside cavity; tie chicken legs together with kitchen string.

3 Place remaining garlic, in single layer, on rack in medium baking dish; place chicken on garlic. Pour the water into dish. Roast chicken, brushing occasionally with pan juices, about 1 hour 20 minutes or until browned and cooked through.

4 Stand chicken on platter, covered with foil, 15 minutes before serving with roasted garlic.

tip Forty cloves may sound like a lot of garlic, but you will be surprised at how mild and creamy the garlic becomes after roasting for such a long period of time.

serving suggestion Serve with roasted potatoes.

ROASTED CHICKEN WITH HERB STUFFING

prep + cook time 2 hours 15 minutes **serves** 4
nutritional count per serving 35.9g total fat (14.4g saturated fat); 2437kJ (583 cal);
19.4g carbohydrate; 45g protein; 1.9g fibre

1.5kg (3-pound) whole chicken
15g (½ ounce) butter, melted
herb stuffing
1½ cups (105g) stale breadcrumbs
1 stalk celery (150g), trimmed,
    chopped finely
1 small white onion (80g), chopped finely
1 tablespoon finely chopped fresh
    flat-leaf parsley
2 teaspoons finely chopped fresh
    sage leaves
1 egg, beaten lightly
30g (1 ounce) butter, melted

1 Preheat oven to 200°C/400°F.
2 Make herb stuffing.
3 Remove and discard any fat from cavity of chicken. Rinse chicken inside and out with water. Pat dry cavity and skin with absorbent paper. Fill cavity of chicken with stuffing, fold over skin to enclose stuffing; secure with toothpicks. Tie legs together with kitchen string.
4 Place chicken on oiled wire rack in large baking dish. Half-fill baking dish with water – it should not touch the chicken. Brush chicken with butter; roast 15 minutes.
5 Reduce oven to 180°C/350°F; bake further 1½ hours or until chicken is cooked through, basting occasionally with pan juices. Stand chicken 10 minutes before serving.

herb stuffing Combine ingredients in bowl.
tip To achieve a delicious crispy chicken skin, make sure the surface has been dried thoroughly. Basting the chicken during roasting also helps the skin to brown and keeps the chicken moist.
serving suggestion Serve with roasted potatoes tossed in chopped fresh flat-leaf parsley.

ROASTED BACON-WRAPPED QUAIL WITH MUSCAT SAUCE

prep + cook time 45 minutes **serves** 4

nutritional count per serving 20.9g total fat (7.7g saturated fat); 1689kJ (404 cal); 12.4g carbohydrate; 33.8g protein; 3.6g fibre

4 quails (780g)

1 medium lemon (140g)

20g (¾ ounce) butter

4 rindless bacon slices (260g)

⅓ cup (80ml) muscat

250g (8 ounces) green beans

½ cup (125ml) chicken stock

155g (5 ounces) fresh muscatel grapes, halved

1 Preheat oven to 200°C/400°F.

2 Discard necks from quails. Wash quails under cold water; pat dry with absorbent paper.

3 Halve lemon; cut one lemon half into four wedges. Place one lemon wedge and a quarter of the butter inside each quail. Tuck legs along body, wrapping tightly with bacon slice to hold legs in place.

4 Place quails in medium flameproof baking dish; drizzle with 1 tablespoon of the muscat and juice of remaining lemon half. Roast, uncovered, about 25 minutes or until quails are browned and cooked through. Remove quails from dish; cover to keep warm.

5 Meanwhile, boil, steam or microwave beans until tender; drain. Cover to keep warm.

6 Return flameproof dish with pan liquid to heat, add remaining muscat and stock; stir until sauce boils and reduces to about ½ cup. Add grapes; stir until heated through.

7 Serve quail on beans topped with sauce.

tip Quail is a small delicately flavoured game bird, related to the pheasant and partridge, and ranges in weight from 250g (8 ounces) to 300g (9½ ounces).

pork

ROAST LEG OF PORK WITH APPLE SAUCE

prep + cook time 2 hours 40 minutes (+ standing) **serves** 8
nutritional count per serving 34g total fat (9.7g saturated fat); 2976kJ (712 cal);
27.4g carbohydrate; 71.9g protein; 4.1g fibre

2.5kg (5-pound) boneless
   pork leg roast, rind on
2 tablespoons olive oil
1 tablespoon sea salt flakes
6 medium potatoes (1.2kg), quartered
2 tablespoons olive oil, extra
2 tablespoons each fresh sage leaves and
   fresh rosemary leaves
apple sauce
3 large green apples (600g)
½ cup (125ml) water
1 teaspoon white sugar
pinch ground cinnamon

1 Preheat oven to 220°C/425°F.
2 Score pork rind with sharp knife; rub with oil, then salt. Place pork in large shallow baking dish. Roast, uncovered, 20 minutes.
3 Reduce oven to 180°C/350°F; roast, uncovered, about 2 hours.
4 Meanwhile, combine potato with extra oil and herbs in large bowl. Place in single layer on oven tray. Roast, uncovered, about 35 minutes.
5 Make apple sauce.
6 Stand pork, covered loosely with foil, 10 minutes before slicing. Serve pork with apple sauce and sage potatoes.
apple sauce Peel and core apples; slice thickly. Place apples and the water in medium saucepan; simmer, uncovered, about 10 minutes or until apple is soft. Remove pan from heat; stir in sugar and cinnamon.
tip You can use boneless pork shoulder roast instead of the leg roast, if you like.

PORK LOIN WITH SPINACH AND PANCETTA STUFFING

prep + cook time 2 hours **serves** 10

nutritional count per serving 25.7g total fat (7.1g saturated fat); 2458kJ (588 cal); 40.3g carbohydrate; 47g protein; 1.8g fibre

4 slices white bread (120g)
2 tablespoons olive oil
1 medium brown onion (150g),
   chopped coarsely
3 cloves garlic, crushed
6 slices pancetta (90g), chopped coarsely
100g (3 ounces) baby spinach leaves
¼ cup (35g) roasted macadamias,
   chopped coarsely
½ cup (125ml) chicken stock
2kg (4-pound) boned pork loin
plum and red wine sauce
1½ cups (480g) plum jam
2 tablespoons dry red wine
⅔ cup (160ml) chicken stock

1 Preheat oven to 200°C/400°F.

2 Remove and discard bread crusts; cut bread into 1cm (½-inch) cubes. Heat half the oil in large frying pan; cook bread, stirring, until browned and crisp. Remove croûtons from pan.

3 Heat remaining oil in same pan; cook onion, garlic and pancetta until onion browns lightly. Stir in spinach; remove from heat. Gently stir in croûtons, nuts and stock.

4 Place pork on board, fat-side down. Horizontally slice through thick part of pork, without cutting whole way through. Open out pork to form one long, fairly flat piece; press stuffing mixture along short end of pork. Roll pork to enclose stuffing, securing with kitchen string at 2cm (¾-inch) intervals.

5 Place rolled pork on wire rack in large shallow baking dish. Roast, uncovered, about 1¼ hours or until cooked through.

6 Meanwhile, make plum and red wine sauce.

7 Serve sliced pork with sauce and steamed asparagus, if you like.

plum and red wine sauce Bring ingredients to the boil in small saucepan. Reduce heat; simmer, uncovered, 10 minutes or until sauce thickens slightly.

tip When you order the pork loin, ask your butcher to leave a flap measuring about 20cm (8 inches) in length to help make rolling the stuffed loin easier.

HONEY MAPLE GLAZED BAKED HAM

prep + cook time 1 hour 20 minutes **serves** 10
nutritional count per serving 18.7g total fat (6.7g saturated fat); 2930kJ (701 cal);
36.6g carbohydrate; 97.5g protein; 0g fibre

½ cup (180g) honey
½ cup (125ml) maple syrup
½ cup (110g) firmly packed light brown sugar
2¼ cups (560ml) water
7kg (14-pound) cooked leg of ham

1 Preheat oven to 180°C/350°F.

2 Stir honey, syrup, sugar and ¼ cup of the water in small saucepan over heat until sugar dissolves. Bring to the boil; remove from heat, cool 10 minutes.

3 Cut through rind of ham 10cm (4 inches) from the shank end of the leg. To remove rind, run thumb around edge of rind just under skin. Start pulling rind from widest edge of ham, continue to pull carefully away from the fat up to the shank end. Remove rind completely. Score across the fat at about 3cm (1¼-inch) intervals, cutting through the surface of the fat (not the meat) in a diamond pattern.

4 Pour the remaining water into large baking dish; place ham on oiled wire rack over dish. Brush ham all over with honey maple glaze. Roast ham, uncovered, 1 hour or until browned, brushing frequently with glaze during cooking.

tip Use the rind from the ham to cover the cut surface; this will keep the ham moist during storage.

serving suggestion Serve with a salad of asparagus, shelled fresh peas, witlof, mixed salad leaves and a little olive oil.

AMERICAN-STYLE SPARE RIBS

prep + cook time 2 hours 35 minutes (+ refrigeration) **serves** 8
nutritional count per serving 17.2g total fat (4.1g saturated fat); 2107kJ (504 cal); 42.1g carbohydrate; 44g protein; 2.2g fibre

3.5kg (7 pounds) american-style pork spare ribs, in slabs

barbecue sauce

2¼ cups (560ml) tomato sauce (ketchup)
1½ cups (375ml) cider vinegar
⅓ cup (80ml) olive oil
½ cup (125ml) worcestershire sauce
¾ cup (165g) firmly packed light brown sugar
⅓ cup (95g) american-style mustard
1½ teaspoons cracked black pepper
3 fresh red thai (serrano) chillies, chopped finely
3 cloves garlic, crushed
¼ cup (60ml) lemon juice

1 Make barbecue sauce.
2 Place slabs of ribs in large deep baking dish; brush both sides of each slab with sauce. Pour remaining sauce over slabs. Cover; refrigerate overnight, turning slabs occasionally in the sauce.
3 Preheat oven to 160°C/325°F.
4 Drain slabs; reserve sauce. Divide slabs between two wire racks over two large shallow baking dishes. Roast, covered, 1½ hours, brushing with sauce every 20 minutes. Turn slabs midway through cooking time.
5 Increase oven to 220°C/425°F. Uncover slabs; bake in hot oven, brushing frequently with sauce, until slabs are browned and cooked through, turning after 15 minutes.
6 Place remaining sauce in small saucepan; bring to the boil. Reduce heat; simmer, stirring, about 4 minutes or until sauce thickens slightly.
7 Using scissors, cut slabs into portions of two or three ribs; serve ribs with hot barbecue sauce.
barbecue sauce Bring ingredients to the boil in medium saucepan. Remove from heat; cool before brushing over ribs.
tip To save on cleaning time, line the base of each dish with baking paper.
serving suggestion Serve with potato salad or coleslaw.

ASIAN-SPICED ROASTED PORK BELLY

prep + cook time 1 hour 35 minutes (+ refrigeration) **serves** 6
nutritional count per serving 37.9g total fat (12.7g saturated fat); 2195kJ (525 cal);
10.3g carbohydrate; 32.6g protein; 2.4g fibre

1kg (2 pounds) pork belly, skin on, boned
½ cup (125ml) chinese cooking wine
   (shao hsing)
¼ cup (60ml) soy sauce
1 tablespoon tamarind concentrate
2 tablespoons honey
½ teaspoon sesame oil
4cm (1½-inch) piece fresh ginger (20g),
   chopped finely
3 cloves garlic, crushed
2 teaspoons five-spice powder
1 star anise
1 dried long red chilli
1 teaspoon sichuan pepper
3 cups (750ml) water
900g (1¾ pounds) baby buk choy,
   halved lengthways

1 Place pork in large saucepan of boiling water; return to the boil. Reduce heat; simmer, uncovered, about 40 minutes or until pork is cooked through. Drain.
2 Meanwhile, combine wine, soy, tamarind, honey, oil, ginger, garlic, five-spice, star anise, chilli, pepper and the water in large bowl. Add pork; turn to coat pork in marinade. Cover; refrigerate 3 hours or overnight.
3 Preheat oven to 220°C/425°F.
4 Place pork, skin-side up, on wire rack in large shallow baking dish; reserve marinade. Pour enough water into baking dish to come halfway up side of dish. Roast, uncovered, about 30 minutes or until browned.
5 Meanwhile, strain marinade into small saucepan; bring to the boil. Boil, uncovered, about 20 minutes or until sauce reduces to about 1 cup.
6 Boil, steam or microwave buk choy until just tender; drain.
7 Serve pork on buk choy with sauce.

ROASTED PORK NECK WITH CHERRIES

prep + cook time 1 hour 30 minutes (+ refrigeration) **serves** 4
nutritional count per serving 23.7g total fat (7.8g saturated fat); 2065kJ (494 cal);
31.7g carbohydrate; 35.8g protein; 1.4g fibre

2 teaspoons sichuan peppercorns
2 teaspoons sea salt
700g (1½-pound) pork neck
1 tablespoon olive oil
2 cloves garlic, sliced thinly
2 cinnamon sticks
2 star anise
5cm (2-inch) piece fresh ginger (25g),
    sliced thinly
¼ cup (60ml) plum sauce
¾ cup (180ml) oyster sauce
¼ cup (60ml) light soy sauce
¾ cup (180ml) rice wine vinegar
1 cup (250ml) water
1 cup (250ml) water, extra
400g (12½ ounces) canned seeded black
    cherries in syrup

1 Combine peppercorns and salt in mortar and pestle; grind until coarse. Score pork skin in diagonal pattern; rub skin with oil then pepper mixture.
2 Combine garlic, cinnamon, star anise, ginger, sauces, vinegar and the water in medium bowl. Add pork, ensuring rind is not submerged. Cover; refrigerate 3 hours.
3 Preheat oven to 220°C/425°F.
4 Drain pork; reserve marinade. Place pork on oiled wire rack in medium shallow baking dish. Pour 1 cup reserved marinade into dish. Roast, uncovered, 20 minutes.
5 Reduce oven to 200°C/400°F. Add the extra water to dish; roast, uncovered, about 40 minutes or until pork is cooked.
6 Add cherries and syrup to dish; roast, uncovered, 5 minutes. Remove pork from dish, cover; stand 10 minutes before slicing. Skim and discard fat from sauce.
7 Serve pork with cherries and sauce.

vegetables

ROASTED TRUSS TOMATOES WITH CRISPY BASIL

prep + cook time 20 minutes **serves** 8
nutritional count per serving 2.5g total fat (0.3g saturated fat); 134kJ (32 cal);
1.5g carbohydrate; 0.4g protein; 1.2g fibre

500g (1 pound) baby vine-ripened
  truss tomatoes
2 cloves garlic, sliced thinly
1 tablespoon olive oil
2 teaspoons balsamic vinegar
vegetable oil, for deep-frying
⅓ cup loosely packed fresh basil leaves

1 Preheat oven to 180°C/350°F.
2 Place tomatoes on oven tray; pour combined garlic, oil and vinegar over tomatoes. Roast, uncovered, 10 minutes or until tomatoes soften.
3 Meanwhile, heat vegetable oil in small saucepan; deep-fry basil, in batches, until crisp.
4 Serve tomatoes sprinkled with basil.

FENNEL AND POTATO GRATIN

prep + cook time 1 hour 35 minutes **serves** 8
nutritional count per serving 29.7g total fat (19.4g saturated fat); 1634kJ (391 cal);
21.7g carbohydrate; 8.1g protein; 3.4g fibre

800g (1½ pounds) potatoes, peeled
2 small fennel bulbs (400g), sliced thinly
1 tablespoon plain (all-purpose) flour
1¾ cups (430ml) pouring cream
¼ cup (60ml) milk
20g (¾ ounce) butter, chopped
¾ cup (90g) coarsely grated cheddar cheese
¾ cup (50g) stale breadcrumbs

1 Preheat oven to 180°C/350°F. Oil deep
2-litre (8-cup) baking dish.
2 Using sharp knife, mandoline or V-slicer,
slice potatoes into 3mm (⅛-inch) slices;
pat dry with absorbent paper. Layer a
quarter of the potato slices into baking dish;
top with a third of the fennel. Continue
layering remaining potato and fennel,
finishing with potato.
3 Blend flour with a little of the cream in
medium jug to form a smooth paste; stir in
remaining cream and milk. Pour cream
mixture over potato; dot with butter.
4 Cover dish with foil; bake about 1 hour or
until vegetables are just tender. Remove foil;
top with combined cheese and
breadcrumbs; bake, uncovered, about
15 minutes or until top is browned lightly.

SPICY ROASTED PUMPKIN, CARROT AND PARSNIP

prep + cook time 45 minutes **serves** 8
nutritional count per serving 10.7g total fat (2.5g saturated fat); 995kJ (238 cal); 28.9g carbohydrate; 4.5g protein; 5.6g fibre

900g (1¾-pound) piece pumpkin,
   unpeeled, sliced thinly
1 tablespoon olive oil
4 large carrots (720g), halved, sliced thickly
2 large parsnips (700g), chopped coarsely
⅓ cup firmly packed fresh flat-leaf
   parsley leaves
¼ cup (40g) roasted pine nuts
spice paste
2 cloves garlic, quartered
1 teaspoon each cumin seeds and
   coriander seeds
½ teaspoon ground cinnamon
1 teaspoon sea salt
1 tablespoon olive oil
20g (¾ ounce) butter
¼ cup (55g) firmly packed light brown sugar
1½ cups (375ml) apple juice

1 Preheat oven to 200°C/400°F.
2 Place pumpkin and oil in large baking dish; toss pumpkin to coat in oil. Roast, uncovered, about 25 minutes or until just tender.
3 Meanwhile, boil, steam or microwave carrot and parsnip, separately, until just tender; drain.
4 Make spice paste.
5 Place vegetables, parsley and nuts in large bowl with spice mixture; toss gently to combine.
spice paste Using mortar and pestle or small electric spice blender, crush garlic, seeds, cinnamon, salt and oil until mixture forms a thick paste. Melt butter in large frying pan; cook paste, stirring, about 3 minutes or until fragrant. Add sugar and juice; bring to the boil. Cook, stirring, about 10 minutes or until spice mixture thickens slightly.

ROASTED BALSAMIC ONIONS AND GARLIC

prep + cook time 1 hour **serves** 4
nutritional count per serving 9.8g total fat (1.4g saturated fat); 702kJ (168 cal); 13.9g carbohydrate; 3.5g protein; 5.6g fibre

2 medium red onions (340g), quartered
2 medium brown onions (300g), quartered
2 bulbs garlic, halved horizontally
2 tablespoons olive oil
1 tablespoon balsamic vinegar
1 tablespoon light brown sugar

1 Preheat oven to 220°C/425°F.
2 Combine ingredients in medium baking dish.
3 Roast, brushing occasionally with pan juices, about 40 minutes or until onions and garlic are tender and caramelised.

ORANGE AND MAPLE GLAZED BABY CARROTS

prep + cook time 25 minutes **serves** 4
nutritional count per serving 17.2g total fat (4.5g saturated fat); 1145kJ (274 cal);
20.8g carbohydrate; 4.1g protein; 7.7g fibre

30g (1 ounce) butter
800g (1½ pounds) baby carrots, trimmed
2 teaspoons finely grated orange rind
¼ cup (60ml) orange juice
2 tablespoons dry white wine
2 tablespoons maple syrup
½ cup (70g) coarsely chopped
   roasted hazelnuts

1 Melt butter in large frying pan;
cook carrots, turning occasionally,
until almost tender.
2 Add rind, juice, wine and syrup; bring to
the boil. Reduce heat; simmer, uncovered,
until liquid has almost evaporated and
carrots are tender and caramelised.
3 Serve carrots sprinkled with nuts.

HASSELBACK POTATOES

prep + cook time 1 hour 30 minutes **serves** 4
nutritional count per serving 22.8g total fat (10g saturated fat); 1463kJ (350 cal);
24.5g carbohydrate; 8.8g protein; 3g fibre

4 medium starchy potatoes (800g),
   halved horizontally
40g (1½ ounces) butter, melted
2 tablespoons olive oil
¼ cup (25g) packaged breadcrumbs
½ cup (60g) finely grated cheddar cheese

1 Preheat oven to 180°C/350°F.
2 Place one potato half, cut-side down, on chopping board; place a chopstick on board along each side of potato. Slice potato thinly, cutting through to chopsticks to prevent cutting all the way through. Repeat with remaining potato halves.
3 Coat potatoes in combined butter and oil in medium baking dish; place, rounded-side up, in single layer. Roast 1 hour, brushing frequently with oil mixture.
4 Combine breadcrumbs and cheese; sprinkle over potatoes. Roast potatoes further 10 minutes or until browned.
tip Desiree or ruby lou potatoes are suitable for this recipe.

BROAD BEAN MASH

prep + cook time 30 minutes **serves** 4
nutritional count per serving 17.9g total fat
(11.3g saturated fat); 1810kJ (433 cal);
44.3g carbohydrate; 18.1g protein; 11.1g fibre

Shell 1kg (2 pounds) fresh broad beans,
discard pods. Boil, steam or microwave
beans until just tender; drain. Peel away
grey-coloured outer shells; blend or process
beans until smooth. Stir in 2 tablespoons
hot pouring cream. Boil, steam or
microwave 1kg (2 pounds) coarsely
chopped potatoes until tender; drain.
Mash potato in large bowl; stir in processed
bean mixture, 40g (1½ ounces) butter and
2 tablespoons hot pouring cream.

CELERIAC PUREE

prep + cook time 35 minutes **serves** 4
nutritional count per serving 14.4g total fat
(9.2g saturated fat); 815kJ (195 cal);
7.4g carbohydrate; 5.2g protein; 8.8g fibre

Bring 2 cups chicken stock to the boil in
medium saucepan; add 1kg (2 pounds)
trimmed, peeled and coarsely chopped
celeriac (celery root), return to the boil.
Reduce heat; simmer, covered, about
30 minutes or until celeriac is tender. Drain.
Blend or process celeriac in batches with
½ cup pouring cream until smooth. Serve
celeriac sprinkled with 1 tablespoon finely
chopped fresh chives.

mash

KUMARA MASH

prep + cook time 30 minutes **serves** 4
nutritional count per serving 8.5g total fat
(5.4g saturated fat); 1024kJ (245 cal);
34.2g carbohydrate; 5.6g protein; 4.3g fibre

Boil, steam or microwave 500g (1 pound)
coarsely chopped potatoes and 500g
(1 pound) coarsely chopped kumara
(orange sweet potato) until tender; drain.
Mash potato and kumara in large bowl until
smooth; stir in 40g (1½ ounces) butter and
¼ cup hot chicken stock.

PERFECT MASHED POTATO

prep + cook time 30 minutes **serves** 4
nutritional count per serving 10.2g total fat
(6.6g saturated fat); 1028kJ (246 cal);
30.1g carbohydrate; 6.7g protein; 3.4g fibre

Boil, steam or microwave 1kg (2 pounds)
coarsely chopped potatoes until tender;
drain. Using the back of a wooden spoon,
push potato through fine sieve into large
bowl. Stir in 40g (1½ ounces) butter and
¾ cup hot milk.
tip Using hot milk instead of cold gives a
creamier mash.

ALMONDS

ground also called almond meal.

ARTICHOKES

hearts tender centre of the globe artichoke; cooked hearts can be bought from delicatessens or canned in brine.

jerusalem neither from Jerusalem nor an artichoke, this crunchy brown-skinned tuber tastes a bit like a water chestnut and belongs to the sunflower family. Eat raw in salads or cooked like potatoes.

BACON SLICES also known as rashers.

BAKING PAPER also called parchment paper.

BAY LEAVES aromatic leaves from the bay tree available fresh or dried; adds a strong, slightly peppery flavour.

BEANS

broad (fava) also called windsor and horse beans; available dried, fresh, canned and frozen.

white a generic term we use for canned or dried cannellini, haricot, navy or great northern beans belonging to the same family, phaseolus vulgaris.

BEEF

eye-fillet also known as beef tenderloin; fine textured, extremely tender and more expensive than other cuts.

gravy boneless stewing beef from shin; slow-cooked, imbues stocks, soups and casseroles with a gelatine richness.

minced also known as ground beef.

rump boneless tender cut taken from the upper part of the round (hindquarter). Cut into steaks, good for barbecuing; as one piece, great as a roast.

scotch fillet cut from the muscle running behind the shoulder along the spine. Also known as cube roll, cuts include standing rib roast and rib-eye.

silverside also called topside roast; the actual cut used for making corned beef.

BEETROOT (BEETS) also known as red beets; firm, round root vegetable.

BICARBONATE OF SODA (BAKING SODA) raising agent.

BREADCRUMBS

fresh bread, usually white, processed into crumbs.

packaged prepared fine-textured but crunchy white breadcrumbs; good for coating foods that are to be fried.

stale crumbs made by grating, blending or processing 1- or 2-day-old bread.

BUTTER use salted or unsalted (sweet) butter; 125g is equal to 4 ounces (one stick) of butter.

CAPERS the grey-green buds of a warm climate (usually Mediterranean) shrub, sold either dried and salted or pickled in a vinegar brine; tiny young ones, called baby capers, are also available both in brine or dried in salt.

CAPSICUM (BELL PEPPER) also known as pepper. Membranes and seeds should be discarded before use.

CELERIAC (CELERY ROOT) tuberous root with knobbly brown skin, white flesh and a celery-like flavour. Keep peeled celeriac in acidulated water to stop it discolouring.

CHEESE

fetta Greek in origin; a crumbly textured goat- or sheep-milk cheese with a sharp, salty taste.

haloumi a Greek Cypriot cheese with a semi-firm, spongy texture and very salty sweet flavour.

CHERRIES, MORELLO sour cherries available bottled in syrup. Used in baking and savoury dishes and are a good match for game.

CHERVIL also known as cicily; mildly fennel-flavoured member of the parsley family with curly dark-green leaves.

CHICKEN

breast fillet breast halved, skinned and boned.

drumstick leg with skin and bone intact.

small chicken (poussin) also called spatchcock; no more than 6 weeks old, weighing a maximum of 500g (1 pound).

tenderloin thin strip of meat lying just under the breast; good for stir-frying.

thigh skin and bone intact.

thigh cutlet thigh with skin and centre bone intact; sometimes found skinned with bone intact.

thigh fillet thigh with skin and centre bone removed.

CHILLI use rubber gloves when seeding or chopping fresh chillies.

green any unripened chilli; also some particular varieties that are ripe when green, such as jalapeño, habanero, poblano or serrano.

long red available both fresh and dried; a generic term used for any moderately hot, long, thin chilli (about 6cm to 8cm long).

thai (serrano) also known as "scuds"; tiny, very hot and bright red in colour.

CHINESE COOKING WINE (SHAO HSING) also called chinese rice wine; made from fermented rice, wheat, sugar and salt with a 13.5% alcohol content. If you can't find it, replace with mirin or sherry.

CLOVES dried flower buds of a tropical tree; can be used whole or in ground form. They have a strong scent and taste so should be used sparingly.

CORIANDER (CILANTRO) also called pak chee or chinese parsley; bright-green-leafed herb with a pungent aroma and taste.

glossary

CORNFLOUR (CORNSTARCH)
available made from corn or
wheat; used as a thickening
agent in cooking.

COUSCOUS a semolina flour and
water dough is sieved then
dehydrated to produce
minuscule even-sized pellets of
couscous; it is rehydrated by
steaming or with the addition of a
warm liquid and swells to three or
four times its original size.

CREAM
pouring also called pure or
fresh cream. It has no additives
and contains a minimum fat
content of 35%.

CUMIN also known as zeera or
comino; resembling caraway in
size, cumin is the dried seed of a
plant related to the parsley family.

DUCK whole ducks are available
from specialty chicken shops,
open-air markets and some
supermarkets.

EGGPLANT also called aubergine.

EGGS we use large chicken eggs
weighing an average of 60g
unless stated otherwise in the
recipes in this book. If a recipe
calls for raw or barely cooked
eggs, exercise caution if there is
a salmonella problem in your
area, particularly in food eaten by
children and pregnant women.

FENNEL also called finocchio or
anise; a crunchy green vegetable
slightly resembling celery that's
eaten raw in salads; fried as an
accompaniment; or used as an
ingredient in soups and sauces.
Also the name given to the dried
seeds of the plant which have a
stronger licorice flavour.

FIVE-SPICE POWDER usually a
fragrant mixture of ground
cinnamon, cloves, star anise,
sichuan pepper and fennel seeds.

FLOUR
plain (all-purpose) unbleached
wheat flour is the best for baking:
the gluten content ensures a
strong dough, which produces a
light result.

self-raising all-purpose plain or
wholemeal flour with baking
powder and salt added; make
yourself with in the proportion of
1 cup flour to 2 teaspoons
baking powder.

GARAM MASALA based on
varying proportions of
cardamom, cinnamon, cloves,
coriander, fennel and cumin,
roasted and ground together.
Black pepper and chilli can be
added for a hotter version.

GHEE clarified butter; with the
milk solids removed, this fat has
a high smoking point so can be
heated to a high temperature
without burning.

GOLDEN SYRUP a by-product
of refined sugarcane; pure
maple syrup or honey can
be substituted.

HAM HOCK the lower portion of
the pig's leg; includes the meat,
fat and bone. Most have been
cured, smoked or both.

HARISSA a North African paste
made from dried red chillies,
garlic, olive oil and caraway
seeds; can be used as a rub
for meat, an ingredient in sauces
and dressings, or eaten as a
condiment. It is available from
Middle Eastern food shops and
some supermarkets.

HORSERADISH
cream a commercially prepared
creamy paste consisting of
grated horseradish, vinegar, oil
and sugar.

prepared is preserved
grated horseradish.

**KUMARA (ORANGE SWEET
POTATO)** the Polynesian name
of an orange-fleshed sweet
potato often confused with yam;
good baked, boiled, mashed or
fried similarly to potatoes.

LAMB
backstrap also known as eye
of loin; the larger fillet from a row
of loin chops or cutlets. Tender,
best cooked rapidly: barbecued
or pan-fried.

cutlet small, tender rib chop;
sometimes sold french-trimmed,
with all the fat and gristle at the
narrow end of the bone removed.

fillets fine texture, most
expensive and extremely tender.

leg cut from the hindquarter;
can be boned, butterflied, rolled
and tied, or cut into dice.

minced ground lamb.

rolled shoulder boneless
section of the forequarter, rolled
and secured with string or netting.

shank forequarter leg;
sometimes sold as drumsticks or
frenched shanks if the gristle and
narrow end of the bone are
discarded and the remaining
meat trimmed.

shoulder large, tasty piece
having much connective tissue
so is best pot-roasted or braised.
Makes the best mince.

MAPLE SYRUP maple-flavoured
syrup or pancake syrup is not an
adequate substitute for the
real thing.

MAYONNAISE, WHOLE-EGG
commercial mayonnaise of high
quality made with whole eggs
and labelled as such.

MILK we use full-cream
homogenised milk unless stated
otherwise.

MIXED SPICE a classic spice
mixture generally containing

caraway, allspice, coriander, cumin, nutmeg and ginger, although cinnamon and other spices can be added. It is used with fruit and in cakes.

MUSHROOMS

button small, cultivated white mushrooms with a mild flavour. When a recipe in this book calls for an unspecified type of mushroom, use button.

porcini, dried the richest-flavoured mushrooms, also known as cèpes. Expensive but, because they are so strongly flavoured, only a small amount is required for any particular dish.

swiss brown also known as roman or cremini. Light to dark brown mushrooms with full-bodied flavour; suited for use in casseroles or being stuffed and baked.

MUSTARD

american-style bright yellow in colour, a sweet mustard containing mustard seeds, sugar, salt, spices and garlic. Serve with hot dogs and hamburgers.

wholegrain also known as seeded. A French-style coarse-grain mustard made from crushed mustard seeds and dijon-style french mustard.

OREGANO a herb, also known as wild marjoram; has a woody stalk and clumps of tiny, dark-green leaves. Has a pungent, peppery flavour.

PANCETTA an Italian unsmoked bacon, pork belly cured in salt and spices then rolled into a sausage shape and dried for several weeks.

PAPRIKA ground dried sweet red capsicum (bell pepper); there are many types available, including sweet, hot, mild and smoked.

PASTRY SHEETS ready-rolled packaged sheets of frozen puff and shortcrust pastry, available from supermarkets.

PINE NUTS also known as pignoli; not a nut but a small, cream-coloured kernel from pine cones. They are best roasted before use to bring out flavour.

PORK

american-style spareribs well-trimmed mid-loin ribs.
belly fatty cut sold in rashers or in a piece, with or without rind or bone.

cutlets cut from ribs.

fillet skinless, boneless eye-fillet cut from the loin.

loin chops or roasting cut from the loin.

minced ground lean pork.

neck also called pork scotch, boneless cut from the foreloin.

scotch fillet boneless cut from the foreloin.

shoulder joint sold with bone in or out.

PROSCIUTTO a kind of unsmoked Italian ham; salted, air-cured and aged, it is usually eaten uncooked.

QUAIL related to the pheasant and partridge; a small, farmed game bird ranging in weight from 250g to 300g.

ROSEMARY pungent herb with long, thin pointy leaves; use large and small sprigs, and the leaves are usually chopped finely.

SAGE pungent herb with narrow, grey-green leaves; slightly bitter with a slightly musty mint aroma.

SILVER BEET (SWISS CHARD)

also known, incorrectly, as spinach; has fleshy stalks and large leaves, both of which can be prepared as for spinach.

STAR ANISE a dried star-shaped pod whose seeds have an astringent aniseed flavour; commonly used to flavour stocks and marinades.

TAMARIND found in Asian food shops. Gives a sweet-sour, slightly astringent taste to marinades, pastes and sauces.

THYME has tiny grey-green leaves that give off a pungent minty, light-lemon aroma. Dried thyme comes in both leaf and powdered form.

TURMERIC also called kamin; is a rhizome related to galangal and ginger.

VINEGAR

balsamic originally from Modena, Italy, there are now many balsamic vinegars on the market, ranging in pungency and quality depending on how, and for how long, they have been aged.

rice a colourless vinegar made from fermented rice and flavoured with sugar and salt. Sherry can be substituted.

VEAL

osso buco another name butchers use for veal shin, usually cut into 3cm to 5cm thick slices and used in the famous Italian slow-cooked casserole of the same name.

rack row of small chops or cutlets.

rolled shoulder also called boneless veal shoulder; a whole boneless shoulder that has been rolled and tied. Suits roasting.

scaloppine a piece of lean steak hammered with a meat mallet until almost see-through; cook over high heat for as little time as possible.

schnitzel thinly sliced steak.

WORCESTERSHIRE SAUCE

thin, dark-brown spicy sauce developed by the British when in India; used as a seasoning for meat, gravies and cocktails, and as a condiment.

YOGURT we use plain full-cream yogurt in our recipes unless stated otherwise.

ZUCCHINI also known as courgette; belongs to the squash family. Yellow flowers can be stuffed or used in salads.

conversion chart

MEASURES

One Australian metric measuring cup holds approximately 250ml, one Australian metric tablespoon holds 20ml, one Australian metric teaspoon holds 5ml.

The difference between one country's measuring cups and another's is within a 2- or 3-teaspoon variance, and will not affect your cooking results. North America, New Zealand and the United Kingdom use a 15ml tablespoon. All cup and spoon measurements are level. The most accurate way of measuring dry ingredients is to weigh them. When measuring liquids, use a clear glass or plastic jug with metric markings.

We use large eggs with an average weight of 60g.

DRY MEASURES

METRIC	IMPERIAL
15g	½oz
30g	1oz
60g	2oz
90g	3oz
125g	4oz (¼lb)
155g	5oz
185g	6oz
220g	7oz
250g	8oz (½lb)
280g	9oz
315g	10oz
345g	11oz
375g	12oz (¾lb)
410g	13oz
440g	14oz
470g	15oz
500g	16oz (1lb)
750g	24oz (1½lb)
1kg	32oz (2lb)

LIQUID MEASURES

METRIC	IMPERIAL
30ml	1 fluid oz
60ml	2 fluid oz
100ml	3 fluid oz
125ml	4 fluid oz
150ml	5 fluid oz
190ml	6 fluid oz
250ml	8 fluid oz
300ml	10 fluid oz
500ml	16 fluid oz
600ml	20 fluid oz
1000ml (1 litre)	1¾ pints

LENGTH MEASURES

METRIC	IMPERIAL
3mm	⅛ in
6mm	¼in
1cm	½in
2cm	¾in
2.5cm	1in
5cm	2in
6cm	2½in
8cm	3in
10cm	4in
13cm	5in
15cm	6in
18cm	7in
20cm	8in
23cm	9in
25cm	10in
28cm	11in
30cm	12in (1ft)

OVEN TEMPERATURES

These oven temperatures are only a guide for conventional ovens. For fan-forced ovens, check the manufacturer's manual.

	°C (CELSIUS)	°F (FAHRENHEIT)
Very slow	120	250
Slow	150	275-300
Moderately slow	160	325
Moderate	180	350-375
Moderately hot	200	400
Hot	220	425-450
Very hot	240	475

The imperial measurements used in these recipes are approximate only.

index

Look out for the
BOLD & BRIGHT
mini cookbook range

On sale at selected newsagents and supermarkets
or online at acpbooks.com.au

·TRIPLE TESTED·
·FOR YOUR SUCCESS· EVERY TIME·